On Reflection

Moments, Flight, and Nothing New

Adjoa Wiredu

JACARANDA

TWENTY
in 2020
Black Writers, British Voices

This edition first published in Great Britain 2020
Jacaranda Books Art Music Ltd
27 Old Gloucester Street,
London WC1N 3AX
www.jacarandabooksartmusic.co.uk

A CIP catalogue record for this book is available from the British
Library

ISBN: 9781913090159
eISBN: 9781913090357

Cover image: Adjoa Wiredu, 'Barcelona 2018'
Cover Design: Rodney Dive
Typeset by: Kamillah Brandes

Printed and bound by CPI Group (UK) Ltd, Croydon, CR0 4YY

For Mum

Contents

Moments

Flight

Nothing New

Yam, Tottenham 2015

Sky, Tottenham Marshes 2017

Moments

Pieces of Me

She has sandals that sparkle,
glittery straps face us
as we face wooden handlebars
strapped to the wall.
In the sports hall of a primary school, we wait for the test.

The same sky and, like then,
no writing on the back of the test. No chewing the tops of the borrowed pens.
No looking over the shoulders of the person in front.
I stare down.

The sun falls through the tinted windows onto the floor in patterns.
I watch her feet. From beneath her long skirt I see perfect toes and shiny
silver pieces
winking at me.

Primary School

When I was in primary school, there was a boy in my class called Winston. He drew people. Even at that age we knew there was something special about his sketches. He pressed down hard on pencils, making all of his images dark with detail. He used shading to create the perfect frown or smile, and the round wrinkled pout he consistently drew on illustrations of my face. His large eyes gawked at me from his narrow skinny face as he feathered my mouth. He drew me a lot. And because we were kids and there was nothing else to talk about, it was always just: "Winston likes you." But I don't think he did. I think there was something about my face, my expression, that he liked to draw.

Purple

I was called purple. Not black. Purple. Being the darkest girl in the class, and the darkest black girl in the school, many of the kids thought it was funny to say I was purple. I think it was a boy I fancied who said it first and then it caught on. I remember being upset about it. Upset that I had been singled out. Back then I wasn't picturing a shiny, taut aubergine, plums, grapes or the dark leaves of a smoke bush, the delicate folds of a bearded iris, burgundy-blue. It felt like an insult, like being compared to something unpleasant. Something sore or painful, like a bruise on white skin or problematic gums.

Fly Tipping, 2016

I was asked what I ate at home. The kids at my primary school had backgrounds from a mix of cultures. Many of us were the children of immigrants. Somehow—I guess it wasn't a secret—some of the kids knew that Ghanaians have a dish called fufu and they thought this was funny.

They would ask: "Do you eat fufu?"
When I didn't answer, more insistently: "Do you eat fufu?"
Then hysterical laughing. I hated being asked in that way and I hated having to say: "Yes, I do."

Akos I

The strange shiny mat was stiff and fraying. As it lay flat on the floor, Akosua could see the stains. They looked like drips, splashes of some sort, *tea, coffee?* She was told to spread the blanket onto the mat, place the mattress on top of the blanket and then, finally, the sheets to sleep on. The mattress too had stains, but she felt too weak to wonder what they could be. Her sore feet were barely holding her up as she turned the mattress from its side onto the floor. It landed with a thud, just off the mat. As she bent and manoeuvred the bulky mattress, it slid. She forgot the blanket. Slowly she walked over to the far side of the mattress and pushed it back up against the wall, using all her weight. With a stretch she picked up the blanket, shook it loose and spread it over the plastic mat. For a moment she turned and looked at the room of boxes, tables and dusty wooden chairs. This was her bedroom tonight and maybe for a while. Until she found Kofi.

I Know That Voice

You call out my name and before I look up, I know it's you
I know that voice, the silky tone, the drowsy pace.

You drag your words.
When you say my name
        it   takes   time:

I hear each tone like a jazz song

Saxophone   I turn smiling
                      Ready to walk over,
                      for a hug, to touch

Trumpet   To get a mother's warm kiss

High hat   I don't see you much and I miss you

Trombone   That smile, that deep dirty laugh

You have more wrinkles and you seem tired,
But your eyes twinkle and your cheeks are plump.

You tell me the news and I hold my breath until my eyes are wet.
When you look down at the floor I can't speak: I nod instead.

I want to hug away your troubles, I want to talk away the issues,
the sickness, the dread.

                            (I know I can't)

You ask me about life.
You want to change the subject but I shrug.

I want to sit with you here at the bus stop, as you smoke.
Not waiting for the 341, but right here on this seat, just breathing,

In silence.

Demolition

Afua

The Linley billboard has a Gordon's advert. Whoa, check out this street! Bright green as well, that stands out on there, whoa. They want some attention around here! Is Gordon's any good?
What's this all about? Dirty mattresses here as well, that's four today. It's freezing. 17:40, I'm early.

Call Centre
Supermarket
Exotic Food
Vinh Vu
Guy's Meat Shop

Leading to Whitley Road. Why on earth do some roads have that? Of course it's leading to another road, I don't get it. Maybe I should walk through the park if there aren't too many crazies. Then the meeting. Where's that poster, do I have any left? Oh yeah, here.

Vote
SAY NO TO DEMOLITION. SAY NO TO PRIVATISATION.
SAY NO.

SAY NO?

I should bring this up at The Space. Something for the group to talk about. *Say no? Really?*

"YOU Paki!! Paki!! DID YOU HEAR ME?!"

They're not even Pakistani – those men look like they're Somalian. What the—what is he doing? Why isn't anyone saying anything? How can no one say anything to that man? His face is so red. He's had a drink or two, but still, how is he allowed to say that in public at the bus stop? And those men aren't even from Pakistan. They look sad. *Walk away!* Someone say something. At least the bus is coming. *Get away from that mad man.* Hope he doesn't follow them. Shit. He's off like nothing happened. I told Martin this type of thing happens. Guys like that should be locked up.

Tsk. Another mattress, and if that isn't enough, you all thought you should add the chest of drawers, a random pole, and last night's kebab? Sort it out number 656. What do you all think this is, a big fat rubbish dump? When's the rubbish collection around here anyway? How long do we have to look at this shit?

Barbara

I am so tired. My hip hurts. I better lean forward to help with the pain. This backpack is so heavy but I need my water. That's important. And the toilet roll, and Vaseline. The last time I came to the High Road I forgot… All of that blood. I remember it very well. Everyone watched me. They watched me while I tried to find a tissue for my nose. The blood spoilt my brown coat and those Pizza GoGo people would not even call a cab for me. It can happen at any time and no one will help me. I have to carry my things. I cannot leave my backpack. It is heavy but at least if it happens again, I will be okay. I have to take my small bag with me as well. I need the hospital letters, otherwise I will forget the date like last time. I need my purse, my phone, my keys, my makeup bag;

you never know when the sweat will rub off my makeup. I need to take both bags. I do. Anyway the bus will come soon. It is the bag on my back that feels heavy. Otherwise it will be okay. Once I sit down for a little bit I will be okay. Why don't they have seats at this bus stop? After standing all day I have to come and stand here. Do we not deserve seats who stand all day? I am so tired. I should go to this man and buy avocado while I wait. Where is this bus? I cannot believe how the wind is blowing through this coat. I thought it was going to be warm. My hip. Ooah. I should lean a little bit further. Afua told me to lean a little when it feels like this. What is she—? Oh, she is trying to see if the bus is coming. Something must be coming. It is. Good. Please let it be the 243, please let it be the 243, please let it be...Thank god.

"Where's my phone? Where is it? It was right here!"

Poor woman. Somebody should tell her, there is no need to lose your voice shouting, and no point in crying. *They don't hear you; they don't care.* Ooah. Pick up your bags and come and get on this bus, love. We have all waited long enough. Your phone is gone, love. Come with us.

Afua

"So we've all gathered to decide what to do. I take it you've all seen the leaflets?"

What leaflets? I think he means the *WhatsApp* message about the leaflets. Or maybe he means the posters? I didn't get a leaflet. Shall I tell him? Why are they printing this stuff anyway? Everything around here will be flattened. Why did I even bother to come? David. Yeah, David looks like he's good at these things and at least he will give me some more info that I've been trying to find for mum. He's got a lot of papers there, maybe it's plans. Hope so. I'm sick of the guessing games. Will this place be flattened or what? When can we move to the new block and will mum get any money out of this?

"For those of you who haven't heard, the latest is that the council does not have enough money to buy leaseholders out. I know, I know. Apparently, they plan to decant tenants, but they still need to raise the money for leaseholders. Ha! They don't even know what they're doing!"

Everyone is making noise, but I don't know what this means. Do we have to stay here? What is he talking about? Do we have to stay here?

Red Brick Banana Break

I walk to get a sandwich from the coffee shop. The sandwich and the coffee shop are around the corner.

red-bricks-pushchair-scooter-short red bus

The slope is gentle but uneven. Droopy trees. Curling leaves are starting to cover the ground. My feet crunch a few as I step inside.

grey paint-pale wood-shiny La Marzocco smile-teeth-fringe-hanging light bulbs

Mini stacks:
saucers,
shot glasses,
paper cups.

No sandwiches. I order a soya flat white. Disappointed. Not much of a break without food. Fringe offers a banana. No charge. How lucky. Banana flavoured coffee.

Large table and there's three of us. It's tight. I'm stiff in my coat. Sweating in the sun by the window. My large backpack squashes in with me and touches the thigh of the woman reading to my left. A typist on my right. Soon it's roasting. I'm snug. There's a sigh. She sniffs, it's a blocked nose. Something's wrong with her typing. She stops. Stares at the screen. Looking me over first, my face, my bag, my hands around the cup, the reader talks to the fringe. It fills the small space. We're in the female changing rooms. But we're not because I have coffee and I can't pretend to pack my bag and pull up my tights. I listen.

"What else can I do?"

"It's going to have this thing called The Stack."

"The fruit salad is beautifully arranged all the time. If that's what's important."

Fringe is a talker. Perky. Nice. I look around, zone out. Finish my banana.

The space fills with the sounds of tapping, music, gentle chatter. The sun goes in. I should get back. Up the slope and around the corner.

red brick-short red bus-up the stairs-inside

"The fruit salad is beautifully arranged all the time. If that's what's important."

In Sections

I'm feeling cold, hate the mornings. Too quiet. But I don't want to be looked at. I'm going in that corner. Two coats and still cold. In a minute I'll walk around.

/

I'm paying my council tax bill, right now, before I get another reminder. No privacy at home and no privacy on these computers either! Squashed in like sardines. What is this?

/

I'm going to read this book and play when everyone gets here. Tuesday is the best day of the week. I hope mum packed the treat she promised.

/

I'm re-stacking and re-stacking. I hope I get a moment to read. Is it ever dead in here? Never the afternoon I work, that's for sure.

/

I'm looking for that book Rae said to get. Where is it? B-R-O-O– where's K-M?

/

I need help with this pushchair if I'm to get through those doors. Ah. It's automatic. Great. I'll just need someone to press that thing.

While I sit slurping hot soup

I'm on my way, I listen to you
Your thoughts are
A sound that waits for me to catch up

You pause, notes spill
One on top of the other
The salty cheese on my tongue burns

Jolts me awake
You feel near, everything else is lost
A black hole

I am slowly blowing this hot liquid cold
I listen, concentrate
Like a duvet, I wrap myself in your reverie

Christmas Dinner

I was at a Christmas dinner at an Indian restaurant with five-maybe-six
white colleagues who played a game and asked me to wear a mask
at the end of it. They played it to prove that I didn't know as much as I thought
and they won. They won the game. A selection of questions I couldn't answer.

Their glowing faces. Laughing, happy. Good work.
After a dinner of spicy vegetables, they wanted me to wear a mask.
I smiled and looked away. Paralysis. The lights dim.

I was at a Christmas dinner at an Indian restaurant with five-maybe-six
white colleagues who played a game and asked me to wear a mask
at the end of it. I wanted to pour curry over their heads and watch it drip down
their faces. I thought we were a team. The punishment for that stupid idea
was to make me sit with a mask over my face.

I was at a Christmas dinner at an Indian restaurant with five-maybe-six
white colleagues who played a game and asked me to wear a mask
at the end of it. Simmering, I told them I would wear it later. I didn't.
Two months later I quit.

Red wine in Bordeaux

W
H
O

Oranges

Avocado
Dark chocolate

A
M

Sun dried tomatoes

I
?

Stares

Stories

Vintage furniture

Sunday markets
Gardens

The walk

Sunsets
Violet

Mum's waakye
contentment in my mouth

the hurt of what she said, its acid
turning our friendship

the heaviness of expectation, full-on
exhaustion, can't move

in a year: shaving it all, braiding
curls long, letting out my spring-like
afro hair

watching you closely, copy-cat
movements, thinking off the page,
what a freak

that feeling when I catch the look on
his face as he drives

from that hard red plastic bench by
the house to sitting on a bike seat,
sweaty smelly cyclist

dad's forehead, his creased full lips
the biggest eyes in the room, mum's
cheeks

all there before I was fully me

Who am I?

Summer, Barcelona 2018

⌐ ⌐

i.

When I first came here, I didn't even need to find a job. I had
secured one in the UK. It was one of those schemes so I had no
problem at all. People were saying, how will you find a job? But I
had one before I even left. I'm different from them. I have a British
passport and as soon as I say anything, they can hear my British
accent. It's horrible really because I know I'm different and I can
see that I get special treatment. After twelve years, I am fluent
in Spanish and Italian and I can get by in French. I could get
interviews for international roles and jobs right across Europe if
I wanted. I went into the food business and now I own my own
restaurant.

ii.

She had three cleaning jobs and me. Then she worked at a restau-
rant and learned everything she could about customer service. She
did just about anything and worked with anyone willing to take
her on while she waited for her papers. When I was little she was
too afraid to leave me alone. She took me with her to a few of
her cleaning jobs in the city. I sat and watched as she cleaned the
desks and hoovered the strange, thin carpet. Washing out the dirty
cups and ashtrays, tipping gathered cigarette butts into the black
bag. Repeating the routine at the next desk, and the next. Some
of them were a mess, covered with piles and piles of papers. Mum
dusted around the piles.

iii.

He told me he voted Leave. He said he was listening to the news
and nobody cares about us anymore. The government doesn't care
about health anymore. What could he do? He agreed to go on

BBC Radio 4. My friends listened. I was still in shock. He said the people living in our area are all new, he doesn't recognise anyone anymore. We're Indian for god's sake. Doesn't he understand that there's something wrong with that kind of thinking? They are selling more drugs he said, more than he's ever seen before. He said he was scared, he asked: "Who are these people anyway? Why are they coming here?" I feel like asking, why did *you* come here? He's angry because the government's not helping and he reckons the rest of Europe is pushing them all here. "Why are we the only ones helping?" he says. "If we leave it will be calmer. Things will start to calm down."

⌟ ⌜

Flight

Paris Market, 2017

Akos II

Akosua's dark fingers parted a small area at the front and began to plait the slippery blonde hair of her customer. The customer had a small head and thin, damp strands. *This silky hair will not hold.* Her shoulders were pink and glossy from the sun and her yellow vest was too short for her long body. The central part of her bum covered the small, wooden stool, and the rest of her flesh spilled over it. Her feet were tucked under her for stability and her knees were pressed together. Hunched over and staring into her phone, she still had the concentration and balance for texting. Akosua finished the first row and reached over to the front of her customer's head to part a new line. She angled her body forward to get the next row perfect. Grabbing the hair extension from the table, she fingered another small piece to start. Mame Konado was watching in silence. It was important to get it right if Akosua was to continue working with this group. The only problem was this girl and her thin hair. Kofi had worked hard to get this trial, she could not let him down. Akosua leaned over to begin. Holding a piece of hair between her fingers, in a hurried, brisk motion, she pulled and wrapped the extension around it.

"Excuse me, I'm so sorry but can you please be careful? My scalp is a little delicate. Thanks so much." Akosua chewed the inside of her cheek.

We Ate Fish

He's from a small town near Barcelona and has just returned this summer. He had been living and working in London where he met my boyfriend. We met him near the station at the beach because he promised to take us to a small fish restaurant. It's a day for fish in Barcelona; on a day like this, the heat draws you to the sea. And so, after a little time at the beach: touts trying to get our attention, too many people hanging around getting their toes wet, swimming, eating, we escape up a small street, before and not too far from the main parallel road. We go into a tiny place that's already filled with people, some waiting outside. When they finally find a table for us, tucked in the back, we eat from small plates, stuffing hot pieces of fish, pastry and potatoes into our hungry mouths. He tells us he's still trying to find a job, he's staying with his mother at the moment. He's very attractive even if he's incredibly short. Sea blue eyes and a full, thick, sandy-coloured beard, like a designer wooden brush for scrubbing. He has long hair he tries to keep short but grows so quickly that I know he usually has shoulder-length hair. I think he was wearing a green t-shirt that now makes me think of fresh pea puree and a splash of olive oil. His golden arms are proof that he's had a lot of sun in the last few months. We're meeting him because my boyfriend misses him. They're good friends but they haven't seen each other for ages. When we step out of the restaurant the sun is lower and there's a slight breeze on my bare legs. Bigger bellies than when we walked in, we ask him to walk with us a little. He seems distracted now we've eaten. I wonder if it feels strange to meet us while he's trying to get his life back together and we're on holiday. We should have been ecstatic, we were so looking forward to seeing him, but somehow there's another feeling in the air that I can't put my finger on. Is it when you stay in the bath too long? When it rains on a Sunday afternoon? The aftertaste of before? What was this other feeling, and who was this other character walking with us? I couldn't understand it. When I think about that day now, I mostly think about the food at the restaurant, it was so good.

La Barceloneta

You want me gone
Where can I go?
If I sell you beer
Will you let me stay?

Can I make you drunk
Forget
Change your mind?
I can fit
If you let me

Can I sell you something?
A scarf
A bag
Do you need new shoes?

What can I sell you my friend?
What can you buy?
Do you want a meal?

I have it
I can make you good food
What do you want?

Avoid me tomorrow
Go the other way

If you don't see me, can I stay then?

Figs

dusky, muted colour of blueberries, delicate
ripe bruise, split open
      a newborn baby

lime green light. soft swell, translucent slime
begging to be saved from the sun,   eaten with quick fingers

we walked the hills of northern Italy,
ripe bruise, split open
the sweet filling my nostrils, curling into my empty belly
lime green light. soft swell. hanging heavy

i got to know my new love
merging   watercolours
under a lilac sky, shaded by forest

sharing this fruit —
soft swell, translucent skin
quick fingers —
fused us.

The Storm

After the Sagra, the skies lit up
techno bolt behind hills.

patter-patter-patter-patter
splatter-patter-patter-splatter
heat electric charge, spark
white-flash
one-two-three-four-five

                                        rummmmble-crack-clap

We were scared to drive, jumping over puddles
splatter-patter-patter-splatter
inside, buckles, *pitter-patter-pitter-patter*
wipers *squeal, flap-squeal, flap*
off

shielded by tall trees, dark waving leaves
swerving, under branches swaying
heat electric charge, spark
white-flash

                                        rummmmble-crack-clap

mirror, indicator, screeching right
onto our route out to the city
heat electric charge, spark
white-flash

just above our heads
the large glowing vein
up in the air
taking a breath

                                   rummmmble-crack-clap

air out
focused on the meters ahead, oh-another
heat electric charge, spark
white-flash

                                   rummmmble-crack-clap

streak
my heart, in my throat
waiting for the heart monitor

beep

Light Change

He was dark by traffic amber / pressed on the hedge reaching for eternity / back of a billboard / his feet reaching on tips / breathing in from the sides / down they came / colour wrapped in cello / sunny bunched petals / yellow red shook loose on pavement / as he unwedged his secret stash from behind the metal wall / it rained for the stopping custom-er / his walk down the line in line / out of line still invisible / hoping for tomorrow

Jellyfish, Friuli-Venezia Giulia, 2018

Barbes

Showtime

Grey hoods no hats no hood hats, hood rats. Waving, swaying, moving, being moved. Crowds
walking, passing, side stepping. Into me, shoving
me, pushing me. Guys hanging, pacing, here, there, shouting, looking.
Smiling at you, me,
friends – are we? Try not to smile.

They laugh, hunched.

Standing, passing, exchanging – money, cigarettes, whatever – something.
Clenched fist,
reaching, jumping, placing above, lamppost, rest. It rests
– a hiding spot?

Flying metro overhead, arriving, creaking, stopping. Joining the fun.
This is bravado. Top boys. Favoured few. Hustling on the streets.
Legal corner activity. In view.
For show. Freelance. This is the jungle juggle. Grubby. Lawless.
Rules on the ground.
Belonging. Surviving.

Cocky crowd sectioned off down the stairs at Barbes.
I am waiting at the lights.
I stand at the entrance of Tati.
I stand on the island at Barbes.
I am everywhere. I can see all things, from all angles at the junction of Barbes.

I cross, get through the thick curtains.
It's calm, dark. Quiet.
Eyes adjust, wooden tables, flowers, chandeliers, a bar.

I am scruff. The lost. Searching for a pause.
Up the stairs, lights, large windows, colourful art.
A fireplace, wait to be seated. Another bar, a see-through bar, a bar for show
a bar for showings
and show-offs.

Coffee drinkers to one side, diners to the other – with a view.
A view of the action, below. Lifestreaming.
I sit on green velvet with a binding booklet.
Thick words on thick cards for a thick wallet. Big spender.
I order wine, look down, peer out, catch up.

Plot Boulevard de la Chapelle.
Popcorn sellers, under a bridge, below graffiti, below subtitles.
Old man finds a trolley, tests it by the bins, by the bags of rubbish.
Bags of grey plastics that stick in a heap.
Leaflet shifters, shifting. Touts at speakers' corner, talking, groups smoking.
Head down, break down, I miss the new scene.

– the police turn up, it's a shut-down, a close-up.
Two uniforms, two teens, two grins, two shrugs and no one else. Nothing else.

– a clean stage, no touts, no crowds, a disappearing act.
Police leave, the train departs. Magic.
They all come back, like rabbits pulled from a hat.

– another glass of wine, s'il vous plaît.
I am sitting, looking down, getting comfortable at Brasserie Barbes.
All who get through the bars that turn, turn back.
All who get stuck, shove.
All who chat, know the deal, for real.
All who pause, go up, and enjoy the show.

Barbes, ,2017

Nation

I see you. Tall. Orange hat. Bony oval face. Long
limbs with shiny skin like mine. Black waterproof, zipped up.

I see you ahead. You look lost. Stopping. Starting. Circled by a wall of tiny orange,
blue, white and grey tiles. It's drip drip damp; stale down here.

We all offload and it's loud,
a rush to get the green 9, the turquoise 6,
the blue 2, the red A. For some, it's up the stairs, down
the vault, around the corner, heavy legs shuffle through the long concrete tube–
up more stairs, a walk through the ticket barriers, up the last set of stairs,
then

                                                                                        air.

An easy exit 5. But you stay down here. Punctured.
Lurking in the tunnels, on hold for us. I saw you yesterday and last week. Yesterday
you stopped in the crowd and crouched to fix your lace, looked around and
again behind,
got up, turned and stumbled.

                              'Pardon, pardon,'
                              looking down at the floor.

You had a brown laptop bag but it looked empty, dirty. What's in it?

You walk ahead, slowly, bottom half squashed in the crowd, shuffling.
We turn off and lose a dozen. We drag our feet across the hard floor and up the stairs.
Two armed policemen stand at the barriers and to the side of me now I see you
turn and catch
a glimpse as you walk back through the hollow tunnel.

The Train

somewhere between Vienna and Kraków
you, a train conductor, shouted at me in a language I didn't understand
and kept shouting and shouting
until my eyes stung
cheeks damp
kept shouting
until the other passengers from the local towns spoke
kept shouting
until they helped me understand
that I had to show you my passport
not just my ticket.

Come ti Chiami?

What a pretty name, a little difficult.
You should really come up with something more exotic.
She laughed, I laughed.

Bodrum

Sugababes sugarbabes!
You!

Can I have a picture?

You!
Sugababes sugarbaabes!
Is it you?

Please, a picture?

Italian Class

Nine blokes from West Africa. And me. Squashed into a tiny room for free.
Italian for beginners, for immigrants. Staring at the board we learn how to read job adverts. One of the guys can speak English and Twi. We sit together and chat. He tells me he's just married an Italian girl. He's waiting for his papers and a job.

I don't tell him he's made my week.
I don't tell him he reminds me of Dad, but younger.

I don't ask him if he wants to study.
I don't ask him what he wants to do.

I don't tell him it might take him 40 years.
I don't tell him it'll be many jobs.

I don't ask him if he wants to go back.
I don't want to break the spell.

I don't want to tell, I don't want to ask.
I just want to listen.

It's the me that meets Dad from 40 years ago.
He seems lighter, care-free. Happy.

Once you get there

If you survive
If you hustle
If you duck
If you stay still
If you have the audacity to reach
Above your station

It can take 40 years
Of work
Submission

Then what?
Once you get there, you should be grateful.
Then what?
Once you get there, you should feel it is a privilege when
Eventually, at 63, hobbling to work with your back pain, your children
Will study, get good jobs, do well.
Once you get there, you hope so.

Where do you end up?

Where are you going with that cage young man?
Topless trolley young man
Where do you put it?
When do you stop the fill when it fills?
What corners do you stop for your search?
Where do you rest?

You going up that hill young man?
You got a towel for your sweat?
It slides down your face, down your back
You taking that stuff anywhere special?
What's up there?
Where do you end up?

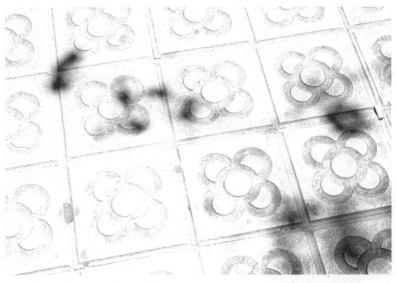

Paving, 2018

⌐   ⌐

Ache
it's too hot
tooth

except on a bike
for a second of sublime breeze
what is her name?
how do I know her?

reply to that email
no, wait for the email
be-care-ful on the way home
the bites—ugh
her name

they slowly enjoy what you take for granted
wine too sweet

must call
put off calling

ah
check in with her
maybe she'll remember
shower again, second time today

red ants
box
talk for one minute
think for one minute
no, listen for one minute

fall over
grey tick, no blue tick
help, help with stuff

Arguing, always arguing
tired

it's going to be okay
it's going to be okay
prints

prints on tiny shorts
teenie wrinkles

such soft skin

⌟ ⌜

Metro

Under-the-path,
An entangled root.
Twisted,
Pushed deep into the ground.
It is the buried dustpan holding the dirt fallen down the cracks, dirt brushed from
the sandy buildings above.

It hides anything that could ruin Haussmann's theatre.
Cherry blossom, celebrated without much thought for the soil
fundamental to its survival.

The living tunnel.
The living root.
The mucky life beneath.

It is the sum of the city. A perfect fusion of rigid ticket-holders and blasé
barrier-jumpers.
It lives in colour. Coated liquorice allsorts stretched across a page;
an edible board game
for children with tiny toy trains.

The Boat Crossing

Swaying walkway
slanted floor
shadows:
the body morphs
into a history paper smudge.

This one knits as we glide.
Surely a winter scarf?
Her hair is covered with a thin white cotton cap.

Wavy hair peeks at the damp front
she frowns, her wool knots mustard.

This one sleeps, her grey cornrows
growing out into a bun. Her face is a distant dream.
She stirs and moves her brown basket bag closer.
We bob.

Nothing New

California Barcelona, 2018

In This Life

i.

A refugee lives above me in my block. She's a single mother to three young children. A few months ago, she had a leak. I only found out when it trickled down into my flat. One wet wall in the boiler room and a puddle in the hallway. It was 7pm. When we went up to find out what had happened, she explained in halting English that the leak started a month ago and had not stopped.

It was cold. The floor was wet. A small bowl was collecting drips from the hallway light and one part of the flat was in complete darkness. It was Good Friday and she said she had been calling the plumber and social services all week but no one had come to help her.

ii.

Feeling around in the dark. We make do with what we have. We work things out for ourselves by asking questions: how is this done? How is that done? How can I do better? When our lives are in the hands of others we simply hope for the best. We wait to hear back. Those questions of 'action' usually come long before we express how we *feel* and then, long before learning how those feelings or experiences can change anything.

iii.

When a baby cries and cries and starts to scream, do we ignore it? Some do. When it screeches and it's uncomfortable to listen, do we ignore it? When it starts straining, scratching at the back of its throat and it's punishment to listen, do we ignore it? Usually, anyone standing within reach picks up the baby. When this happens to an adult and they scream out for help they are boxed in to conform, told to understand there's no one to help. They are forced to stop crying. Stop the damn crying, you should know better.

⌟ ⌜

What are you going to do about it?

Me?
Nothing.
I don't have anything to add. All good.

Thank you.
Really.
Okay.
Sure, understand.
That makes sense.
You're right, of course.
That's interesting.
That's good.
Okay, yes, okay.
I'm listening.
Thanks.
Yes.

Yes, I can do that.
No problem.
Yes, I can find out how to sort that.
No problem.
Yes, I'm available, when's good for you?

Yes.

When I'm angry, I swallow words whole. My jumbled words
expand and trap my mouth shut.

I suppress emotions
I smile
I stare at the wall, out of the window
I change the subject
I agree
I back away
I close the door.

Bully

The false friend.

Their instincts sharp.
A floating fame.
Skilled.
A master of gossip.
They love a good conversation.

Shaming for silence.
King of the world
A glowing position.

They share a little

Affectionate understanding
Chummy, warm orange –

The change is instant
Cold blue, tact to boredom
Yielding to their tempo.

Confused?

They engage, personal.
You divulge.
That's their ticket price, the trip is on you.

They sense it. Feed off it.

The way you stand, smile, talk:

Clues on a billboard
Insecure, lonely
I can take her out.

The school playground
The secondary cool gang
The university wiser, expectant mates rates
The dictator, popular
Boyfriends, bosses, a friend of a friend.

The office banter suggests your incompetence
The minority stain
Lingering implication, segregation leaves you at the mercy
of the ring leader.

The office banter
You know the score, zone out
shut off, play dead.

The Way it Was

Our Price
Wood Green market
half days for shopping city strolls
Wendys, Ravel boy
Pizza Hut, the weekend rut

West Green Road, Bruce Grove
the salon, a weekend wait
brown sticky gel, plaster from hell
holds the sides down well
finish-off right, spray sheen tight

Dalston market before "Oh you mean Ridley Road Market?"
stretch jeans will make you go
blue, red, yellow or green
smooth that bum

In bright puffas, big mummas
gold chains, gold hoops
tucked into large hoods, top deck
Scanning and running
the bus stop, what queue?

Red-rimmed sunglasses, still nodding to
Immature, baggy jeans
Maccy D's, McFlurry
Revising for GCSEs, this is it
Escaping Maths, yearning

for TLC
Left Eye, the best high
dancing on side streets
best mates
back home, strict folks

the finest I'll ever know
the best bit?
the whole lot

It's Complex

Because you only see
what's perfect
I want to tell you all the bad stuff, all the things I want answers to
protest

Because you only see
what's bad
I want to defend us, it, them
mama bear

anything that comes to mind deserves a chance
come on, don't be so judgemental

Because I'm searching, desperate to take it apart and see what's inside
I have a response for everything, you say
even if it's sane, I'll say it's not, let's go
paintballing

anything that comes to mind helps keep this going
come on, keep going, what's your opinion, really? Don't be such a wuss.

Woman at port, 2018

Generation Can-Do

We are told
You can't do this, you can't do that
because you know; you know how it is
for someone like me.
Looking like me, talking without
talking like me, confronting like me –
it is a front.
We missed the depth, the history, our stories.
Because it wasn't expected we didn't disappoint
(*no one will read it anyway*)
We did education for doing
not stretching, pushing, challenging, hoping
until we had no choice.

To ask questions,
attempt to break the rules
stand up, have opinions,
a voice
honour, colour, class-
room. My, your, mind:
that's wealth. Everyone can
progress
process
second generation can-do, be, have, will.

Akos III

Akosua knew something was wrong. She was in the kitchen washing the dishes. Hot water poured from the small shiny tap and into a bowl, soapy bubbles spluttered onto the inside of the sink. She turned off the tap, added more liquid soap in a quick, familiar move, and scrubbed the greasy bowl. The smell of raw beef mixed with sunflower oil and spices lifted from the slippery bowl. It was beginning to nauseate her. With irritation, Akosua added more liquid soap and bit the inside of her cheek. The thick green gloop floated with the bubbles on top of the water and she scrubbed again, this time with less vigour. She could hear the sound of the television, loud but muffled, and she could also hear that Kofi was on the phone.

"It's none of your business, and since when do I have to answer to my little sister?"

She tightened her grip on the sponge and continued to scrub, moving to the edge of the bowl. This was their first meal in this house together, and she was not going to ruin it. She would wait until later to tell him.

London, 2016

I Watch Him

His smart, expanding mind. His warm skin, the colour of date pulp, silky post-polish, just like his father's. He sits reading for hours and hours without taking a break. That, he gets from me. I watch him outside with his friends on that balcony, the tallest, stretching up and jumping a little, a bounce, his chest moves. His lean body from days playing football; he's so strong, still young, I guess. I watch him laughing as he speaks to neighbours, walking slowly on the weekends to get milk for his grandmother. His dark grey tracksuit suits him the best when he's taking time out. I hardly see him on the weekdays but that'll change this summer. I can't wait to speak to him properly, to find out what he loves this year and who he's growing into. I'm looking forward to long stretches of time talking. The way he looks at me for a long time after I've spoken, then he's thinking, smiling that wide spreading of lips. He's about to graduate and then I don't know what he'll do, what I'll do. I watch him speaking on the phone and he looks angry, he's had bad news. He's clenching like I've seen his father do but very quickly, I could've missed it, it's over. Then because he knows I worry like I'm his queen, he kisses me on the cheek and I watch him go up to that room playing bossa nova for the tenth time today. He likes Brazil so much, we should all go again. In just a few months he'll be free from university and I don't know what he'll do, what I'll do. I'll watch him.

Notes

The poems below have been published in the following:

In Sections, The Library Space Residency, Wordpress 2017

Red Brick Banana Break, The Library Space Residency, Wordpress 2017

Nation, Menteur 2017

I Know That Voice, marigoldroadblog, 2017—*in loving memory of Sue*

Metro, Barbes, Nation, Tumblr 2018

Acknowledgments

This is for the hard workers in the diaspora like my parents who have sacrificed to make it possible for me to be here. You got on with it, stood tall, and raised your voices. You embody so many emotions and always strength, even at this unprecedented time. Sometimes sad, sometimes angry, sometimes ecstatic (and dancing in church). Thank you for inspiring the second generation as we keep learning to do the same.

At one point it seemed impossible to suggest that these bits and pieces (the people, the places, and my thoughts in those spaces) were enough to write a collection. I thought my experiences, interpretations of my past and memories were invalid. Because I felt invisible, I thought it would be rejected, and so I explored other people's experiences instead. Here I allowed myself to own my impressions. I dug to understand past connections, I posed questions that led to complex questions, I experienced growth and started to heal. I didn't arrive here alone though. Thank God. I would like to thank so many people who have shown me kindness and patience. And in whom I found time, love, correction, and many discussions.

Thanks to the group of students at Kent University in Paris, The Residency class of 2017. For insightful conversation, feedback, criticism, vulnerability, youthful ideas, and perspective. The opportunity to be in Paris for three months, while being open to a group of young fearless strangers changed a part of me forever. And thanks to our module leader, Adam Biles, who drew me to writers like Perec and brought so many others to my consciousness. To another module leader, Bashir Abu-Manneh, thank you for advising me to 'Do the work.' for encouraging me, pointing me to the right texts and pushing me with your firm challenging words. I also want to thank JIWAR, Barcelona. Many thanks to Mairea for curating the Writers-in-Residence programme. For making me feel safe, welcome and for inspiring me with your world. Thanks to Etsuko Edwards and the team at Stroud Green Library, and to Eleni Markou and team at Coombes Croft Library for the opportunity, guidance and time. Thanks to Deborah Hedgecock at Bruce Castle and Kate Allison at Loven for showing my photography work, all of the advice and support were additional prompts for me to focus on developing my work and consider it from different angles, to value my journey and the personal histories that led me here. Thanks to Arc Artist Residency: Sally, Martina, and to everyone who was part of my experience. Thanks for the opportunity to learn, ponder, research and for that special place it all happened.

I would like to thank the kind people who allowed me to interview them for various projects before I started and while writing this collection. Thanks to Parenthesis Barcelona for considering my work. Thanks to the editorial team and founders of the thoughtful and brilliant Irisi magazine, Desert Rose Lit mag, and then to Cherise Lopes-Baker who came to Jacaranda and helped to edit this collection. Thanks to Valerie Brandes and the entire team at Jacaranda for the most surprising opportunity of my life. And to Akin Schilz, my mentor editor in this project. Your work on this meant and will continue to mean so much to me.

Thanks to Hermione Hoby, that email reply was an incredible seed you planted, it was the trigger I needed in my life at the time. I cannot thank you enough. I hope to do that for someone someday. Allen Ashley's Writing group at Alexandra Park Library, your energy and nudge to write and submit my work was key. Jessica Craig, and Jessica Lott for your encouragement, names of things, places, people I had never heard of and believing in me to go on and find out more for myself. Thanks to Funmi Fetto, for reading, sending me thoughts, for being an inspiration and a quiet wise voice at the beginning of this chapter, which inched me on in my journey. Briony Campbell you rock, thanks for the stirring work you do and for your kindness at an important time.

My deepest gratitude goes to my mother, my bestfriend and my main inspiration. Thanks to the rest of my family for all that you have planted in me. I am encouraged by your wisdom, determination, and our history. Thanks to my love, Filippo for our daily challenging conversations, for support, and for always being there in ways I could not have imagined. Zoya, you would have loved this moment, and I'm sure you would have promptly sent me notes on what I can do better. I miss you.

Mannika, Deepti, Bhumi, Ishani, Sophie, Mairead, Evelyn and all my other friends who have supported the passion for my work, those who have nurtured and loved me throughout the process - you know who you are - thank you.

And it feels important to thank home. It's the place I can't wait to be away from, to breathe for a moment, for clarity, to think about other things. When I'm in transit, as soon as I get a bus, a car, a train, a plane, a boat, it is the place I'm thinking about. It's in every part of me. It's a reminder that I am indeed part of and from somewhere that gives me things to say, to think, to do. Yet still, with so much to say, with so much to do, home hugs, releases me and allows me the space to work out how.

About the Author

Adjoa Wiredu is a writer and artist from London. She writes poetry, personal essays and creative non-fiction about identity. Her work is an attempt to discuss what it means to be a second generation, black British-Ghanaian woman in Europe. It is a quest to understand history, and the small elements in the everyday that trigger personal growth, aspirations and creating new communities.

You can find her bylines at *Irisi Magazine*, Silver Birch Press, *gal-dem*, in *Desert Rose Lit Mag* and Parentheses, Barcelona. In 2018, she engaged in a Walk and Talk research project at Arc Artist Residency; she was a Writer-in-Residence at JIWAR Barcelona, and a recipient of the Heart of Glass professional development bursary. She has an MA in The Contemporary, Kent University, 2017.